LET THEM BUY

The Modern Human-to-Human Sales Playbook

(S)

Staten House

LET THEM BUY

The Modern Human-to-Human Sales Playbook

PHILIP VIVIER

Table of Contents

Introduction

WHY LETTING THEM BUY CHANGES EVERYTHING

Let's face it — the way we sell has changed. Scratch that — the way people **buy** has changed. And if we're being honest, it's been changing for a long time.

This book isn't about learning new tricks to close more deals. It's about shifting your mindset, your message, and your methods to meet buyers where they are now — not where they were ten years ago.

WHAT THIS BOOK IS (AND ISN'T)

This isn't a book about pressure tactics, scripts, or slick closes. It's a book about **opening up** — to new ways of listening, new ways of building trust, and new ways of empowering people to make decisions that feel right for them.

It's not soft. It's smart. Because when you help people buy in a way that honors how they actually make decisions, you don't just make the sale — you make a relationship. And in today's world, that's what lasts.

WHO THIS IS FOR

- ☑ If you're tired of pushing and want to start guiding — this is for you.

- ☑ If you've ever felt like traditional sales advice just doesn't feel right — this is for you.

- ☑ If you lead a team and want to create a culture of trust, not pressure — this is definitely for you.

Whether you're a solopreneur, a seasoned seller, or a sales leader, the Let Them Buy approach will help you:

- ☑ Understand who your buyers really are
- ☑ Communicate in ways that connect
- ☑ Use tools to enhance — not replace — your humanity
- ☑ Teach others to do the same

WHY I WROTE THIS

Back in 2008, I wrote *Stop Selling — Let Them Buy* because I saw something breaking in the sales process: people were exhausted by the pitch. They wanted to feel in control, understood, and respected.

Today, the world is even louder, faster, and more skeptical than ever. And still — people want the same things: clarity, connection, and confidence in their choices.

So I wrote this to help you become the kind of seller the modern buyer actually wants to hear from. The kind that doesn't sell harder — just better.

WHAT YOU'LL LEARN

In the chapters ahead, you'll learn:

- ☑ How to recognize and connect with the four key buyer types

- ☑ How to sell in a remote-first world (without sounding like a robot)

- ☑ How to personalize outreach and follow-ups at scale

- ☑ How to build trust with personality-driven communication

- ☑ How to teach this framework to your team or let me do it for you

You'll find strategies, sample scripts, and real-life language that you can adapt immediately. And if you want to go deeper, there are companion worksheets and even a course you can build — or I can build it for you.

LET'S GET STARTED

Sales doesn't have to be about overcoming objections or wrestling someone into a decision. It can be a conversation — one where both sides win.

So let's begin.

Let's reimagine how sales can feel. Let's rebuild trust, one conversation at a time.

Let's **let them buy**.

—Philip

Chapter 1

WHY THE WORLD DOESN'T WANT TO BE SOLD – AGAIN

The last time you bought something that really mattered — a car, a piece of tech, maybe even a career coaching program or a house — ask yourself: Did you buy it because a salesperson nailed their pitch? Or because you felt understood, in control, and confident in your decision?

Chances are, it was the second one.

In 2008, I wrote *Stop Selling – Let Them Buy* because I saw something breaking in the traditional sales process. People were exhausted by the pitch. They didn't want to be cornered, closed, or convinced. They wanted to be seen, heard, and guided.

Then came 2020. A pandemic. Remote work. Zoom fatigue. Social disconnection. Economic anxiety. And now, even further down the road, a world still recalibrating how to connect, how to trust, and how to decide.

In all of this, one truth has only become clearer:

The pitch is dead. Again.

Today's buyers don't want a closer. They want a co-pilot. Someone who can help them sort through noise, options, overwhelm, and doubt.

THE EMPOWERED (BUT OVERWHELMED) BUYER

Thanks to Google, YouTube, Reddit, ChatGPT, and thousands of expert blogs, the modern buyer knows more than ever. They've researched before they talk to you. They've read the reviews. They've seen your competitors.

But here's the twist: more information doesn't mean more confidence.

In fact, many buyers are paralyzed by it. Too many tabs open, too many options, too many slick marketing messages.

What they're starving for is clarity. And that only comes from someone who listens, guides, and knows when to step back instead of pushing forward.

THE NEW RESISTANCE

Buyers today are tired. Not just of salespeople. They're tired, period.

They're tired of spammy DMs. They're tired of webinars with no value. They're tired of cold calls that assume too much. They're tired of feeling manipulated, even subtly.

Emotionally, they don't have the bandwidth to decipher whether you're being helpful or just clever. Which means that trust has never been more fragile — or more powerful.

They want real. They want safe. They want honesty.

They don't want to be sold. Again.

WHAT SALES NEEDS NOW

We are no longer in the Age of Persuasion. We are in the Age of Permission.

Sales needs a new model — or rather, we need to return to what always worked best: empathy, clarity, and alignment.

The average person sees thousands of brand messages every day — emails, popups, social posts, and sponsored content all trying to convince them to do something. The modern buyer isn't just overwhelmed; they're trained to tune it all out.

That's why the best salespeople today aren't "selling" in the traditional sense. They're guiding. They're curating. They're clarifying. Instead of pushing a pitch, they're making space for a decision.

Sales today isn't a contest — it's a collaboration.

In the chapters ahead, we're going to revisit what it means to sell like a human. We'll talk about personality types. We'll explore the difference between pitching and partnering. And we'll show how the best salespeople today aren't pushy, polished closers.

They're guides. They're teachers. They're trusted voices in a noisy world.

And most importantly, they know that when you let people buy, they do.

Welcome back to the conversation.

chapter 2

THE POST-COVID BUYER MINDSET

Before COVID-19, buyers were already evolving. They were more informed, more skeptical, and more self-directed than ever before. But the pandemic didn't just speed things up — it rewired the way people make decisions. It stripped things down to what matters. It amplified what we fear and what we value.

And it created a new kind of buyer: one who is more protective of their time, their energy, and their trust than ever before.

FROM TRANSACTION TO TRANSFORMATION

Before 2020, most buyers were still open to persuasion. They tolerated a certain level of salesmanship. But after the world was turned upside down, people started asking harder questions:

- ☑ Is this worth my money?

- ☑ Is this worth my time?

- ☑ Will this make my life better?

- ☑ Will this make me feel safe, smart, seen, or supported?

Buyers aren't just looking for transactions now. They're looking for transformation. They're not just buying a product or service — they're buying a feeling, a future, a shift in their reality.

If your offer, your energy, or your message doesn't align with that deeper need, they're out.

SCARCITY OF ENERGY, NOT JUST MONEY

Salespeople have long focused on cost objections. But what many still miss is this:

Today's buyers aren't just protecting their wallets. They're protecting their bandwidth.

Post-COVID buyers are:

- ☑ Emotionally exhausted

- ☑ Zoom-fatigued

- ☑ Overwhelmed with decisions

- ☑ Navigating hybrid or remote work

- ☑ Dealing with uncertainty on every front

Their mental load is heavy. Their tolerance for complexity is low. Which means your sales process can't afford to feel like another task — it has to feel like relief.

You don't just have to sell something valuable. You have to make buying it feel easy, safe, and energizing.

SAFETY FIRST: EMOTIONAL AND PRACTICAL

COVID shook our sense of control. And in the absence of control, people crave safety. Safety in buying means:

- ☑ No bait and switch

- ☑ No pressure

- ☑ Clear expectations

- ☑ Transparent pricing

- ☑ Honest conversations

This is where trust becomes your currency. Not hype. Not charm. Not cleverness.

If your prospect feels safe, they stay in the conversation. If they feel even slightly tricked, they vanish.

Trust is no longer a luxury — it's the cost of entry.

THE RISE OF SELF-SELLING

Post-COVID buyers often prefer to make decisions without ever speaking to someone. They want:

- ☑ Access to information without a gatekeeper

- ☑ Case studies and testimonials that feel real

- ☑ Pricing that doesn't require a demo to reveal

- ☑ Control over their timeline

It's not that they don't want help — it's that they want control.

That doesn't mean salespeople are obsolete. It means you need to be a facilitator, not a barrier. You need to support the self-sell without interrupting it.

Give them room. Give them support. Let them self-direct and be ready to step in when they invite you.

MEET THEM WHERE THEY ARE

There is no going back to "normal" selling.

The new buyer mindset is:

- ☑ Guarded but curious

- ☑ Hopeful but cautious

- ☑ Independent but overloaded

They may not need you at the start. But if you show up right — with respect, clarity, and patience — they'll welcome you at the moment they need help.

Your job is not to break down the wall. Your job is to knock gently, listen fully, and make it easier for them to say yes — not because you pushed, but because it finally felt right.

A NEW ERA OF CONNECTION

This chapter isn't just about understanding your buyer. It's about respecting their journey.

Because when they feel that, they'll come to you. Not because you sold them. But because you let them buy.

And in a post-COVID world, that shift — from persuasion to permission — is what separates the noise from the trusted voice.

Let that voice be yours.

chapter 3

TRUST IS THE NEW CURRENCY

In today's sales landscape, trust isn't a soft skill. It's the whole deal.

People don't buy because of flashy features or polished scripts. They buy because they trust:

- ☑ The product will do what it says.

- ☑ The person selling it actually cares.

- ☑ The process won't waste their time or energy.

Trust is no longer earned in long lunches or slick demos. It's earned in the micro-moments:

- ☑ How fast you respond.

- ☑ How clearly you communicate.

- ☑ How much pressure you don't apply.

THE FRAGILITY OF MODERN TRUST

Post-COVID, post-clickbait, post-fake-everything, buyers are more skeptical than ever. They expect proof. They smell B.S. instantly. And they carry the emotional memory of being burned.

Trust has become fragile but powerful. When you earn it, people act fast. When you lose it, you don't get a second shot.

In a world of deep fakes, filters, and AI-generated everything, *real* stands out. Buyers can sense when someone's showing up with sincerity versus someone showing up with a script.

TRUST > RAPPORT

Sales training has long taught us to "build rapport." Ask about the weather. Compliment their background. Small talk your way into connection.

But modern buyers can sniff out fake rapport instantly. What they crave instead is authentic alignment:

- ☑ Do you understand their problem?

- ☑ Can you speak their language?

- ☑ Are you listening or just waiting to pitch?

Trust isn't charm. It's clarity. Trust isn't chemistry. It's consistency.

Instead of rapport, think *resonance*. Can your message land in a way that feels personal, not personalized by a CRM? That's what modern buyers crave.

TRANSPARENCY IS TRUST IN ACTION

Want someone to trust you? Be clear. Be direct. Be real.

Share your pricing. Explain your process. Admit what your product doesn't do. That kind of honesty is rare. Which is why it stands out.

When buyers see it, they relax. And when they relax, they buy.

Transparency signals safety. It shows you're not hiding anything. It tells your buyer, "You're in control, not me."

Trust thrives in the absence of pressure. Trust grows in the presence of options. Trust locks in when your buyer feels seen, not steered.

THE TRUST TIMELINE

Trust doesn't have to take weeks or months. In today's digital world, it can be earned quickly — but only if you show up right.

Here's how it often plays out:

1. A buyer visits your site. First impressions form in seconds.

2. They see a testimonial that actually feels human, not scripted.

3. They chat with you or a rep who listens instead of pitching.

4. They feel control over their decision.

5. Trust clicks into place.

Notice how none of this involves a pitch deck or a product demo.

It's not about convincing. It's about removing fear.

You don't need to "win them over." You need to not scare them away.

WHAT KILLS TRUST?

- ☑ Vague answers
- ☑ Dodging questions
- ☑ Delaying pricing
- ☑ Overpromising
- ☑ Overselling
- ☑ Faking urgency

If you're not honest about what you *can't* do, they won't believe what you say you *can*.

When a buyer senses even a hint of deception, they don't get mad — they disconnect. And when they disconnect, they don't tell you. They just disappear.

TRUST AS A DIFFERENTIATOR

In markets crowded with noise, gimmicks, and AI-written nonsense, trust is your edge.

Make your message clear. Make your process simple. Make your tone human.

When you do, you become memorable. Not because you were louder. But because you were real.

Trust converts faster than persuasion. Trust retains longer than discounts. Trust earns referrals that scripts never will.

In a world that's tired of being sold, being real is what sells.

And when you lead with trust, you don't just get customers — you earn believers, buyers, and brand advocates.

Because when people feel safe with you, they don't just buy. They come back. And they bring their friends.

chapter 4

HOW TO CONNECT IN A WORLD THAT SWIPES LEFT

We live in a world of fast scrolls and short attention spans. People swipe past hundreds of messages every day. They're not just ignoring ads — they're ignoring anything that doesn't feel instantly relevant, real, or respectful.

So how do you connect in a world that's trained to tune out?

You don't chase. You don't charm. You connect by cutting through the noise with something that still feels rare: genuine attention.

THE DEATH OF GENERIC

Templates are easy. Scripts are scalable. AI can write an email faster than you can blink.

But the modern buyer has a filter. If your outreach sounds like it could have been sent to anyone, they'll treat it like it was meant for no one.

Personalization isn't a first name merge tag. Connection isn't a subject line hack.

It's relevance. It's timing. It's intention.

Buyers crave content that sounds like it was written for them, not to them. When you show that you've done your homework and you respect their time, you earn the opportunity to engage.

THE POWER OF BEING PRESENT

Being present means more than just being "on" a Zoom call. It means:

- ☑ Listening fully without prepping your next line.
- ☑ Watching their facial cues, not your notes.

☑ Responding to what's said, not what you expected.

In a remote, digital-first world, being present is your superpower.

Because when you're present, they feel it. And when they feel it, they open up.

Presence creates pause. And in that pause, connection happens.

ASK, DON'T ASSUME

Most salespeople jump to solutions. Great ones start with better questions.

Questions like:

☑ "What's the biggest frustration you're dealing with right now?"

☑ "What's worked in the past — and what hasn't?"

☑ "If we could remove one headache for you, what would it be?"

These aren't gimmicks. They're invitations. And when you ask with genuine curiosity, people lean in.

Buyers are used to being talked *at*. When you ask well — and actually care about the answer — you flip the script.

LEAD WITH EMPATHY, NOT AUTHORITY

In a world full of noise, people crave safety. And safety starts with feeling understood.

You don't have to be the expert in the first 30 seconds. You just have to be the person who actually gets it.

Empathy doesn't mean being soft. It means being smart enough to know that understanding someone is more powerful than impressing them.

Buyers will choose someone who listens over someone who lectures — every time.

RESPECT THE SCROLL

Every message you send competes with 1,000 others. So earn their attention.

- ☑ Be brief.
- ☑ Be clear.
- ☑ Be human.

Subject lines like "Quick question" or "Following up again" are easy to ignore. Try instead:

- ☑ "Saw this and thought of you."

- ☑ "Is this still a priority for you?"

- ☑ "Can I make this easier?"

If you're interrupting someone, do it with care. Interrupt like a friend would — not like a funnel would.

CONNECTION IS THE NEW CONVERSION

Forget tactics. Forget tricks.

If you want to win in a world that swipes left on almost everything, you have to earn the right to stay on screen.

You do that not by selling better. But by connecting better.

Because in this game, the real edge isn't knowing the perfect close.

It's making sure they don't want to swipe past you in the first place.

Connection converts. Empathy engages. And relevance earns the right to continue the conversation.

When you lead with those, you stop being another notification.

You become a welcomed conversation.

Chapter 5

READING THE ROOM OVER ZOOM

Sales used to happen in boardrooms, coffee shops, and conference halls. Now it happens in tiny boxes on a screen, often with dogs barking, toddlers crashing, or notifications pinging in the background.

Welcome to the world of virtual selling.

While it may seem harder to connect over Zoom, the truth is: you can still build deep trust and read the room — even if the room is a screen.

You just have to learn how to pay attention to the new cues.

THE NEW BODY LANGUAGE

In person, we read posture, eye contact, and physical energy. Online, those cues still exist — they just show up differently:

- ☑ Are they engaged or distracted?

- ☑ Are they nodding, or are they stiff?

- ☑ Do they lean in when you speak?

- ☑ Are their eyes scanning (reading), or are they locked on you (listening)?

You're not just watching their face. You're watching for presence.

Also note their environment. Are they multitasking? Constantly muting and unmuting? Are they turning their camera off during key parts of the conversation? These are signals — and often, calls for a different kind of engagement.

ENERGY SPEAKS FIRST

Even with perfect lighting and crisp audio, your energy speaks before your words do.

Are you calm or frantic? Are you trying to connect, or trying to convince? Are you fully present, or running a mental script?

When your energy is grounded, warm, and confident — your buyer feels it. Even through a screen.

Your energy sets the tone. Set it with intention.

DON'T PERFORM. PARTNER.

Many salespeople go into Zoom calls trying to put on a show: polished, perfect, practiced.

But people don't want a performer. They want a partner.

That means:

- ☑ It's okay to pause and think.

- ☑ It's okay to admit when you need to circle back.

- ☑ It's powerful to ask, "How is this landing with you?"

Great Zoom calls feel like co-creation, not persuasion.

TECHNOLOGY IS NOT THE OBSTACLE. YOU ARE.

Yes, Zoom can be clunky. Yes, it's harder to feel someone's vibe through a webcam.

But it's not the tool that blocks connection. It's the approach.

If you treat the call like a transaction, it will feel transactional. If you treat it like a chance to serve, it becomes relational.

Your camera and mic are tools. The connection comes from your intention.

Practical Ways to Read the Room Virtually

- ☑ Ask early: "What do you hope we walk away with today?"

- ☑ Check in often: "Is this tracking with what you need?"

- ☑ Watch reactions: Use visual cues (eye contact, posture shifts, head tilts)

- ☑ Listen for tone shifts: If their voice goes flat, you may be losing them

- ☑ Use your screen wisely: Don't overload with slides. Use visuals to support, not dominate

- ☑ Notice micro-delays: Are they taking longer to respond? That could signal confusion or disengagement

- ☑ Invite silence: Don't rush to fill every pause. Sometimes the best insight surfaces when you give space

END LIKE A HUMAN

Many sales calls end with a flurry of next steps or a rushed goodbye.

Try instead:

- ☑ "What stood out to you from today?"

- ☑ "Was there anything we didn't get to that you were hoping to?"

- ☑ "What would be most helpful from me next?"

And always — always — thank them for their time. In a world of screen fatigue, attention is the new luxury.

BONUS: USE VIDEO FOR FOLLOW-UP

One underused but powerful tool is asynchronous video. A short, thoughtful follow-up using Loom or Vidyard can:

☑ Reinforce key points

☑ Show you listened

☑ Give a face and tone to your words

In a world of typed text and auto-responses, a 45-second video that's human and specific? That cuts through.

MAKE THE ZOOM ROOM FEEL LIKE A REAL ROOM

Connection doesn't require a handshake. Trust doesn't require a whiteboard.

It just requires that you show up fully, listen generously, and treat that little square on the screen like a sacred space.

Because when you do that, you don't just stand out.

You get invited back.

chapter 6

REBUILDING YOUR SALES ENERGY AFTER BURNOUT

L et's be honest: selling today is exhausting.

Between nonstop Zooms, rising quotas, endless follow-ups, ghosted emails, and juggling work-life boundaries that no longer exist, sales professionals everywhere are tired. Not just physically, but emotionally.

And if you're tired, burned out, or questioning whether you still have "it" in you to show up, you're not alone.

This chapter is about what to do when your tank is empty — and how to refuel it in a way that's sustainable.

BURNOUT ISN'T JUST A PRODUCTIVITY PROBLEM

You might think burnout is about poor time management, lack of discipline, or too much hustle. It's not.

Burnout often comes from a mismatch between what you're doing and what fuels you.

In sales, that mismatch often looks like:

- ☑ Pretending to be "on" when you're not

- ☑ Chasing leads you don't believe in

- ☑ Pushing products you're not aligned with

- ☑ Working with clients who drain you

Your brain knows when you're out of alignment. And it fights back with fatigue, cynicism, and detachment.

SALES REQUIRES ENERGY, NOT JUST STRATEGY

You can have the best script, the best funnel, and the best offer in the world — but if your energy is off, your results will be too.

People don't just buy your product. They buy your energy. They buy your belief. They buy your presence.

If you're not sold on you, they won't be either.

So before you fix your pipeline, fix your state.

SIGNS YOU NEED A RESET

- ☑ You dread every call, even with great prospects

- ☑ You're going through the motions, not really listening

- ☑ You're snapping at objections instead of exploring them

- ☑ You feel numb when you close a deal

- ☑ You're constantly comparing yourself to others

These aren't signs of weakness. They're signals for a reset.

HOW TO REFILL THE TANK

1. **Reconnect with Purpose**

   Remind yourself why you started. Who do you help? What changes when they say yes? If your answer doesn't move you anymore, you might be in the wrong seat.

2. Sell to People You Like

If your best customers energize you, find more like them. Build a pipeline that reflects your favorite kind of person, not just your biggest paycheck.

3. Protect Your Boundaries

Turn off Slack. Say no to late-night follow-ups. Block your calendar. You're not available 24/7, and you shouldn't be.

4. Create Before You Consume

Start your day by writing a note to a client. Journaling. Planning your outreach. Don't let the first thing you see be someone else's win on LinkedIn.

5. Celebrate Small Wins

Burnout thrives when nothing feels like progress. Did someone say, "This was helpful"? That counts. Did you follow up on a tough lead? That counts.

REST IS A REVENUE STRATEGY

We're trained to think rest is indulgent. In sales, it's essential.

When you rest, your creativity returns. Your empathy resets. Your confidence rebuilds.

You don't need more hustle. You need more space to remember who you are when you're not selling.

Because when you show up full, you sell from overflow. And when that happens, burnout becomes less of a threat and more of a reminder: you're human first.

And so are the people you're selling to.

chapter 7

TOOLS THAT HELP YOU HELP OTHERS (WITHOUT BEING A ROBOT)

Sales tech is everywhere. CRM systems. Email automation. LinkedIn trackers. AI copywriters. Chatbots. Sequences. Calendly links. Slides. Video messages.

And yes, they can help.

But when they replace you, instead of amplify you, buyers feel it.

This chapter isn't about ditching your tools. It's about using them to serve, not to sell. To connect, not to control. To scale trust, not shortcuts.

THE PURPOSE OF TOOLS

The best tools help you:

- ☑ Stay organized

- ☑ Personalize at scale

- ☑ Follow up with care

- ☑ Keep promises

- ☑ Show up consistently

But they should never:

- ☑ Replace real conversation

- ☑ Assume instead of ask

- ☑ Prioritize volume over value

- ☑ Make people feel like data points

If your tools make your job easier but your buyer's experience worse, you're using them wrong.

AUTOMATE FOR EFFICIENCY, NOT FOR DISTANCE

Automation is powerful when it saves time. Dangerous when it saves effort at the cost of humanity.

You can automate:

- ☑ Meeting scheduling
- ☑ Follow-up reminders
- ☑ Post-call recaps
- ☑ Nurture sequences with real value

But don't automate:

- ☑ First impressions
- ☑ Relationship-building
- ☑ Problem-solving

Buyers know when they're in a sequence. And they act accordingly.

PERSONALIZATION THAT FEELS PERSONAL

True personalization is more than just name drops and company references. It's showing that you did your homework and understand what matters.

Try:

- ☑ Referring to a specific post they made

- ☑ Mentioning something they said in a webinar

- ☑ Connecting over shared values, not just pain points

Use your tools to capture insights, not just trigger templates.

USE AI TO SUPPORT, NOT SPEAK

Tools like ChatGPT, Grammarly, and CRM assistants are incredible for helping with:

- ☑ Drafting first versions

- ☑ Brainstorming angles

- ☑ Summarizing long notes

- ☑ Suggesting follow-up content

But don't let AI become your voice. Use it to enhance your message, not replace your message.

AI should save you time — not steal your authenticity.

STACK YOUR TOOLS WITH INTENTION

You don't need more tools. You need the right ones that do their job without creating noise.

Ask yourself:

- ☑ Does this help me show up better?

- ☑ Does this create clarity for my prospect?

- ☑ Does this reduce friction or just add features?

Less tech. More intention.

KEEP THE HUMAN AT THE CENTER

Technology will keep evolving.

The real question is: will you?

Your tools should support the human-to-human experience. That means your buyer should feel:

- ☑ Heard, not herded

- ☑ Guided, not gamed

- ☑ Respected, not rushed

Because in the end, your tech stack might be impressive.

But if you forget to be human, no tool can save the sale.

BONUS: MAKE TECH YOUR SIDEKICK, NOT THE STAR

When used wisely, tech can boost your best traits:

- ☑ Use CRM notes to remember birthdays or key interests

- ☑ Send a quick video message instead of a long email

- ☑ Use real-time analytics to time your outreach when it matters most

Smart tools + sincere humans = scalable trust.

And in a world flooded with automation, being thoughtfully human is the ultimate competitive edge.

chapter 8

BUYING IN THE DIGITAL AGE

We used to think about customers in simple categories: job title, budget, need.

Then came personality typing, which added depth and nuance to how we connect. And that skill — being able to recognize, adapt to, and communicate with different personality types — is more valuable than ever.

But today, personality type alone isn't enough. People are more complex, more self-aware, and more diverse than any one model can define.

To create meaningful buying experiences today, we need to support the whole person — their personality, their story, and their situation.

BEYOND THE BUYER PERSONA

Forget the flat customer profiles. Real people carry full identities:

- ☑ Cultural backgrounds

- ☑ Neurodivergence

- ☑ Gender perspectives

- ☑ Personal goals

- ☑ Work trauma

- ☑ Communication preferences

Today's buyers want to be seen not just as decision-makers, but as multidimensional humans navigating a noisy, uncertain world.

Your role isn't to decode all of that perfectly. Your role is to show up with humility, curiosity, and flexibility to meet people where they are.

PERSONALITY TYPES STILL WORK — AND STILL MATTER

Your original method still matters. Understanding personality cues helps you:

- ☑ Adapt your pace

- ☑ Choose better language

- ☑ Predict responses

- ☑ Ask better questions

When layered with empathy and cultural awareness, personality typing becomes a powerful tool — not to label people, but to better serve them.

Because someone might show up as a Driver but be a burned-out Driver with trust issues from a toxic workplace. They may appear to be a Nurturer but carry guardedness from being overlooked in past roles.

Understanding their personality is the beginning — not the end — of the conversation.

WHOLE-PERSON COMMUNICATION

Communication today is emotional labor. It's not just what you say — it's how and when you say it.

It means:

- ☑ Reading tone, not just words
- ☑ Respecting pace and boundaries
- ☑ Recognizing when someone is masking or hiding
- ☑ Knowing when to suggest, and when to pause

This is especially true when working with neurodiverse buyers or those with different cultural expectations around communication.

It also means showing flexibility. Some people need more time. Others want bullet points. Some want to vent before they decide. Others need you to stay out of the way while they think.

SAY LESS. ASK MORE.

To support whole-person decision-making, get better at drawing them out:

☑ "How do you usually make decisions like this?"

☑ "What do you wish people understood better about your role?"

☑ "What's going on behind the scenes that might impact this?"

These questions do more than move the sale forward. They invite trust.

They show the buyer that you're not just trying to check boxes — you're trying to understand.

INCLUSION BUILDS TRUST

Inclusion isn't a buzzword. It's a business advantage.

When people feel seen, heard, and respected for who they are, they engage more deeply. That means:

☑ Avoiding assumptions

☑ Checking your language

☑ Making space for neurodiverse communication styles

☑ Being okay with discomfort if it means deeper connection

This also includes your sales collateral and digital touchpoints. Are your slides readable for everyone? Are your intake forms inclusive in language? Do your visuals reflect diverse buyers?

It's not about being perfect. It's about being intentional.

BUYING IS PERSONAL — ALWAYS

People don't separate who they are from what they buy. Even in B2B, emotion and identity play a role.

If someone's job is on the line, they'll be cautious. If they've been burned before, they'll be guarded. If they're overwhelmed at home, they'll crave clarity and ease in your process.

What you're selling may be a product or service — but what they're buying is peace of mind, a solved problem, or relief from friction.

YOU DON'T NEED TO BE A PSYCHOLOGIST. JUST BE HUMAN.

You won't always get it right. But when your effort is real, people feel it.

You don't need to understand every nuance of identity and personality to create a better experience. You just need to show that you care. That you're listening. That you're willing to slow down and meet them, not manage them.

Because when you treat your customers like whole people, they show up fully. And when they show up fully, they don't just buy.

They trust. They refer. They come back.

UP NEXT

We'll revisit the four core personality types — the Drivers, Analysts, Connectors, and Supporters — and explore how each of them buys, what earns their trust, and how to meet them on their terms in today's noisy world.

chapter 9

THE DRIVER – DIRECT, DECISIVE, AND RESULTS-FOCUSED

Drivers are action-oriented decision-makers. They're quick to assess value, direct in their communication, and focused on outcomes. In my original book, I described them as the people who want to win — and that hasn't changed.

But in today's world, where attention is scarce and skepticism is high, Drivers have evolved. They're still focused on results, but they've also become more discerning about who earns their time.

HOW DRIVERS BUY NOW

Drivers want to move fast, but they don't want to be rushed. They want control, but they don't want to waste time on unnecessary details. They'll appreciate your confidence — but only if it's backed by clarity.

Today's Drivers are:

- ☑ Less patient with fluff or ambiguity

- ☑ More protective of their time and calendar

- ☑ Interested in who else has succeeded with your product — and how quickly

- ☑ Not afraid to walk away if you're not direct

WHAT BUILDS TRUST WITH A DRIVER

- ☑ Respect their time. Be brief, clear, and well-prepared.

- ☑ Speak in outcomes, not features.

- ☑ Present a strong point of view, but back it up with proof.

- ☑ Give them options, not ultimatums.

- ☑ Focus on speed, control, and measurable impact.

Say this: "Here's the most direct way we can solve that."

Not this: "Let me tell you a bit more about us first."

WHAT TURNS THEM OFF

- ☑ Overexplaining

- ☑ Being vague or non-committal

- ☑ Long stories before getting to the point

- ☑ Passive language like "we hope to" or "you might consider"

If you try to charm a Driver without substance, you'll lose them fast.

QUESTIONS THAT WORK WITH DRIVERS

- ☑ "What's your ideal timeline to see a result?"

- ☑ "What would success look like to you — in measurable terms?"

- ☑ "Would it be beneficial if I walked you through the most efficient path forward?"

These questions position you as a partner in execution —

not just a vendor with ideas.

HOW TO FOLLOW UP WITH A DRIVER

- ☑ Get to the point quickly

- ☑ Summarize clearly in bullet points

- ☑ Remind them of outcomes, not steps

- ☑ Keep tone confident and action-oriented

Example: Subject: Quick Recap & Action Plan Here's what we covered:

1. You need X done by Y.

2. We can deliver that in Z days.

3. Here's the next step to keep things moving.

DRIVERS UNDER STRESS

Even high-achieving Drivers experience burnout, especially in today's relentless environment. When stressed, they can become more abrupt, more controlling, and less trusting.

They may:

☑ Demand tighter deadlines

☑ Interrupt more often

☑ Push harder for guarantees

This isn't about ego. It's about pressure. If you can stay grounded and respond with calm confidence, you become the steady hand they didn't know they needed.

MODERN EXAMPLES OF DRIVER BUYERS

Think of leaders like Carlos Alcaraz or Barbara Corcoran. They're bold, fast-moving, direct, and outcome-driven. They expect their teams (and vendors) to keep up. They don't want fluff. They want to know:

☑ Will it work?

☑ How fast?

☑ What's the ROI?

FINAL THOUGHT

Drivers don't want the journey. They want the destination. When you meet their clarity with decisiveness — and their speed with structure — they not only buy.

They lead the charge to bring others along.

Coming up next: the Analyst. Slower to decide, but fiercely loyal once they do.

Chapter 10

THE ANALYST — CAUTIOUS, LOGICAL, AND DETAIL-DRIVEN

If Drivers buy fast and lean into instinct, Analysts do the opposite. They buy slow — on purpose.

Analysts want to get it right. Their confidence comes not from your enthusiasm, but from their own understanding. They don't buy because you made a strong pitch. They buy because your solution made sense.

HOW ANALYSTS BUY NOW

Today's Analysts are more empowered than ever. They've done their research before you showed up. They've already looked at your competitors. They've read the case studies, scanned the fine print, and spotted what you didn't say.

Their biggest concern? Making a wrong decision.

Analysts today:

- ☑ Value logic over emotion
- ☑ Need time to digest, not just hear
- ☑ Expect transparency and documentation
- ☑ Are less responsive to urgency tactics
- ☑ Cross-reference multiple data points before deciding
- ☑ Are highly sensitive to gaps between claims and evidence

They're not dragging their feet — they're protecting their judgment and reputation. They want to avoid risk, and they often serve as the internal "fact-checker" on their team.

WHAT BUILDS TRUST WITH AN ANALYST

- ☑ Be methodical and clear in your explanations

- ☑ Show your math: timelines, costs, outcomes

- ☑ Provide written summaries and resources

- ☑ Encourage them to ask questions (and give them space to think)

- ☑ Share proof and processes, not just results

- ☑ Offer references, use cases, or performance metrics

- ☑ Align your language to their need for accuracy, not excitement

Say this: "Here's how the numbers break down, and why it works."

Not this: "You just have to trust me on this."

WHAT TURNS THEM OFF

- ☑ Pressure to act quickly

- ☑ Gimmicky sales language or emotional hype

- ☑ Vague promises

☑ Overpromising or skipping details

☑ Lack of preparation or disorganized materials

☑ Rushing the process or interrupting their analysis

Analysts will sense a gap between confidence and credibility — and they'll hesitate. They don't trust enthusiasm; they trust evidence.

QUESTIONS THAT WORK WITH ANALYSTS

☑ "What data would you need to feel confident moving forward?"

☑ "Would it help to see how we've handled similar situations?"

☑ "Is there anything that feels unclear or unproven at this point?"

☑ "What's your typical decision-making process for projects like this?"

☑ "Do you want to review this in writing before our next step?"

These questions tell them: It's okay to ask. It's okay to take your time. And more importantly, you're not afraid of their scrutiny.

HOW TO FOLLOW UP WITH AN ANALYST

- ☑ Recap your conversations with clarity and structure

- ☑ Attach links, references, or spreadsheets

- ☑ Offer additional documentation without pressure

- ☑ Reinforce transparency, not urgency

- ☑ Keep tone respectful, concise, and logically ordered

Example: **Subject: Detailed Recap + Resources**

Here's a summary of everything we covered, with the requested breakdowns attached. Let me know what other data would help.

1. Primary goals identified

2. Key deliverables discussed

3. Timeline proposal

4. Supporting materials linked

Let me know if you'd like a walkthrough of any section.

ANALYSTS UNDER STRESS

When under pressure, Analysts may:

- ☑ Become more perfectionistic

- ☑ Ask more clarifying questions

- ☑ Delay decisions for more information

- ☑ Become more sensitive to missing details

Recognize that this isn't avoidance — it's protection. When you validate their need to process, you build enormous trust.

Statements like:

- ☑ "I understand you want to get this right."

- ☑ "Let's slow this down and make sure everything's aligned."

...can go a long way.

MODERN EXAMPLES OF ANALYST BUYERS

Think of people like Bill Gates or Elon Musk — analytical, exacting, and unafraid to ask the hard questions. They thrive on logic and don't jump to conclusions. They are disciplined decision-makers who want:

- ☑ Data-backed insights
- ☑ Low risk, high clarity
- ☑ Thoughtful pacing

They may not be vocal with praise, but once they commit, they're loyal.

FINAL THOUGHT

Analysts don't buy the pitch. They buy the proof.

And when they do buy, they become your most loyal advocates — because they didn't say yes lightly. They said yes because it made sense, stood up to scrutiny, and delivered.

Coming up next: the Connector. Warm, enthusiastic, and driven by human energy.

chapter 11

THE CONNECTOR – ENTHUSIASTIC, RELATIONAL, AND DRIVEN BY ENERGY

Where the Analyst leans on logic, the Connector leans on connection. They want to like you — and want to feel like you like them, too.

In my first book, Connectors were people-first. That hasn't changed. But today's Connectors are more tuned in than ever to authenticity. They can spot fake warmth from a mile away. In a world of automation and AI, genuine human energy is their magnet.

HOW CONNECTORS BUY NOW

Connectors are drawn to relationships, stories, and shared excitement. They want to feel good about the decision — and even better about the person guiding them through it. They don't want a transaction. They want a conversation.

Today's Connectors:

- ☑ Want to feel emotionally safe with you

- ☑ Are sensitive to tone, warmth, and enthusiasm

- ☑ Will follow a trusted recommendation before researching on their own

- ☑ Look for brands (and people) that align with their values

- ☑ Need to believe that buying this will feel good — emotionally, socially, and ethically

Their biggest fear? Feeling foolish or rejected.

WHAT BUILDS TRUST WITH A CONNECTOR

- ☑ **Warmth.** Be enthusiastic, not robotic

☑ **Personal connection**. Use names, remember details, follow up with heart

☑ **Transparency — not perfection**. Be real about the process

☑ **A sense of partnership**: "we're in this together"

☑ **Testimonials and social proof with a human touch**

☑ **Energetic tone and presence** — they respond to emotional cues

Say this: "I really enjoyed our chat — you're exactly who we love working with."

Not this: "Let's get this signed today to lock in pricing."

WHAT TURNS THEM OFF

☑ Cold, transactional tone

☑ Rushed pitches with no space for rapport

☑ Overly formal or stiff language

☑ Lack of emotional acknowledgment (especially when they share a concern)

- ☑ Sales interactions that feel one-sided, impersonal, or mechanical

Push too hard, and they'll shut down — even if they like the product.

QUESTIONS THAT WORK WITH CONNECTORS

- ☑ "What made you smile when you first came across this?"

- ☑ "What kind of support feels good to you during a decision like this?"

- ☑ "Who else is part of the conversation, and how can we make them feel good about this too?"

- ☑ "When you think about the outcome, what would make this a win emotionally?"

These questions open doors to connection — and reassure them you care.

HOW TO FOLLOW UP WITH A CONNECTOR

- ☑ Use a warm, expressive tone

- ☑ Add a personal detail to show you remembered them

☑ Keep it light, positive, and human

☑ Invite conversation — don't just send data

☑ Offer something thoughtful, like a curated video, article, or resource that reflects their personality or values

Example: Subject: So great talking with you — here's what's next!

> Hey [Name],
>
> I pulled together a few highlights based on what you shared — and included that article you mentioned you loved. Take a peek when you get a minute, and let me know what feels good. I've got your back. ☺

CONNECTORS UNDER STRESS

When under pressure, Connectors may:

☑ Seek emotional reassurance

☑ Need extra check-ins or encouragement

☑ Second-guess their instincts if they feel unsupported

☑ Withdraw from conversations that feel too transactional or rushed

Support them by being steady, kind, and present. Phrases like:

☑ "I want you to feel good about this — no pressure at all."

☑ "We can take this at your pace. You matter more than the timeline."

...can bring them back into the conversation.

MODERN EXAMPLES OF CONNECTOR BUYERS

Think of someone like **Dwayne "The Rock" Johnson** — warm, expressive, emotionally attuned, and unapologetically himself. Connectors like Jack lead with heart and influence others by being relatable, funny, and full of humanity. They seek:

☑ Alignment with personal values

☑ Stories that inspire

☑ People who make them feel good and seen

When they believe in you, they become your loudest advocates — referring, reposting, and spreading the word out of pure enthusiasm.

FINAL THOUGHT

Connectors don't just buy the product. They buy the person behind it.

And when you show up with sincerity, warmth, and real connection, they'll not only buy — they'll become your most vocal advocates.

Next up: the Supporter. Steady, loyal, and slow to move — but powerful once they do.

chapter 12

THE SUPPORTER – LOYAL, THOUGHTFUL, AND STEADY

Supporters are the heart of any team — and often the quiet backbone of the buying process. They're loyal, thoughtful, and slow to trust. But once they do, they stay with you.

In my first book, Supporters were described as steady, harmony-seeking, and resistant to change. That's still true. But now they're navigating a world full of noise, uncertainty, and aggressive sales tactics — and it's made them even more cautious, even more intentional.

HOW SUPPORTERS BUY NOW

Supporters don't want flash. They want comfort. They don't want pressure. They want reassurance. They want to be sure — about you, your intentions, and your reliability.

Today's Supporters:

- ☑ Take longer to make decisions
- ☑ Need time to feel emotionally and practically safe
- ☑ Are highly loyal once onboarded
- ☑ Prefer familiar, low-risk options
- ☑ Will prioritize relationships over bargains
- ☑ Respond best to slow, steady, consistent engagement

Their biggest concern? Making a disruptive or regrettable decision.

Supporters often act as internal influencers behind the scenes. They may not speak up in group calls, but their opinion carries weight with decision-makers. Dismissing or overlooking them is a mistake. Win their trust, and they'll champion you quietly but powerfully.

WHAT BUILDS TRUST WITH A SUPPORTER

- ☑ **Patience.** Let them take their time.

- ☑ **Reassurance.** Revisit their concerns without pushing.

- ☑ **Familiarity.** Remind them of your reliability and track record.

- ☑ **Consistency** in tone, messaging, and follow-up.

- ☑ **Proof** that you'll still be there after the purchase.

- ☑ **Kindness.** They respond to warmth, not pressure.

Say this: "There's no rush — I'm here whenever you're ready."

Not this: "Spots are filling fast, and we don't want you to miss out."

WHAT TURNS THEM OFF

- ☑ Pushy or rushed language

- ☑ Abrupt changes in tone or process

- ☑ Lack of follow-through

- ☑ Being made to feel like they're behind or wrong

- ☑ Overly technical or aggressive sales approaches

They'll ghost rather than confront. And they won't come back if they feel overwhelmed.

QUESTIONS THAT WORK WITH SUPPORTERS

- ☑ "What's most important to you in making this decision?"

- ☑ "What would help this feel like the right pace for you?"

- ☑ "How can I support you without adding pressure?"

- ☑ "Who else will this impact, and how can we help make it feel good for them too?"

These questions show care — not control.

HOW TO FOLLOW UP WITH A SUPPORTER

- ☑ Keep tone calm, warm, and steady

- ☑ Revisit any concerns with kindness

- ☑ Offer next steps without deadlines

- ☑ Emphasize reliability and partnership

- ☑ Include reassuring language like "I'm here" or "whenever you're ready"

EXAMPLE: SUBJECT: JUST CHECKING IN — NO RUSH

Hi [Name],

I just wanted to check in and see how things are sitting with you. No pressure at all — I'm just here if anything new comes up or if you'd like to talk through next steps at your pace.

Appreciate your thoughtful approach — we really value working with people like you.

Warmly,
[Your Name]

SUPPORTERS UNDER STRESS

When Supporters feel anxious or overwhelmed:

- ☑ They may withdraw quietly

- ☑ They can become overly agreeable, then back out later

- ☑ They may fixate on small details as a way to regain control

- ☑ They avoid conflict, so silence doesn't mean consent — it means uncertainty

Your role is to:

- ☑ Check in gently

- ☑ Ask how they're feeling about things

- ☑ Reaffirm that there's no pressure

- ☑ Celebrate even small steps forward

Let them feel safe, and you'll earn their long-term trust.

MODERN EXAMPLES OF SUPPORTER BUYERS

Imagine someone like **Keanu Reeves** — steady, grounded, reliable, and kind. Supporters like Tom don't rush. They care deeply about integrity, calm energy, and feeling like they're part of something good. They value:

- ☑ Consistency

- ☑ Long-term relationships

☑ Brands that take care of their people

☑ Quiet professionalism over loud marketing

When you earn their trust, Supporters become your most dependable repeat buyers and low-key brand advocates. They may not shout from the rooftops, but they'll quietly tell the people who matter.

FINAL THOUGHT

Supporters don't make fast moves. They make lasting ones.

If you respect their process and provide calm, consistent care, they'll not only buy — they'll stay. And in a world full of one-click decisions, that kind of long-term trust is gold.

Next: How to adjust your outreach, sales decks, and follow-up sequences to speak to each type — without writing four different strategies from scratch.

chapter 13

ONE MESSAGE, FOUR RECEIVERS – PERSONALIZING WITHOUT STARTING FROM SCRATCH

Now that you understand the four personality types — the Driver, Analyst, Connector, and Supporter — it's time to answer the practical question:

How do I adjust my outreach, sales decks, and follow-up sequences to connect with each personality... without reinventing the wheel every time?

The answer? **Build one flexible strategy that adapts at the edges.** Think of your sales materials as modular — with key moments tailored to match who's in front of you.

WHY ONE-SIZE-FITS-ALL FAILS

Most companies create materials for the average buyer. But when your "average" message hits a Driver, it's too slow. When it hits a Supporter, it's too aggressive. When it hits an Analyst, it's too vague. And when it hits a Connector, it's too dry.

That doesn't mean you need four versions of every slide deck or email.

It means you need **core content** that adjusts on delivery.

MODULAR MESSAGING: THE SMART WAY TO ADAPT

Think of your outreach like a playlist. You've got the main tracks — but depending on your audience, you remix a few songs.

Here's how:

1. Outreach Messages (Email, DM, or Voicemail)

Base Structure:

- ☑ Hook (why you're reaching out)

- ☑ Value (how you can help)

- ☑ Invite (next step)

Now Adjust It:

Type	Hook	Value Angle	Invite Style
Driver	"Cut to the chase..."	Fast ROI, control, impact	"Quick call to outline fastest path?"
Analyst	"Saw your recent review..."	Logic, case studies, clarity	"Happy to send a breakdown for you to review."
Connector	"Loved your recent post!"	Human connection, shared values	"Would love to connect if it feels aligned."
Supporter	"Hope things are calm on your end"	Trust, reassurance, consistency	"No pressure — here if helpful."

2. Sales Decks & Presentations

Don't build four decks. Build one, and adjust **your framing** as you deliver.

Anchor Points to Flex:

- ☑ **Opening Slide:** Start with what matters most to them

- ☑ **Data Slides:** Expand or simplify based on type

- ☑ **Case Studies:** Pick ones that match tone (metrics vs. story)

- ☑ **Call to Action Slide:** Match the pacing

Type	Lead With...	Emphasize...	Avoid...
Driver	Outcomes & timeline	Fast execution, wins	Overviews, drawn-out intros
Analyst	Process & data	Details, logic, documentation	Urgency tactics, vagueness
Connector	Values & people	Stories, enthusiasm	Overly formal tone

Type	Lead With...	Emphasize...	Avoid...
Supporter	Partnership & support	Reassurance, low pressure	Abrupt tone or big change

3. Follow-Up Sequences

This is where tone and timing matter most. You don't need four campaigns — you need **four flavors** of the same one.

Type	Tone	Timing	Language to Use
Driver	Confident, direct	Fast	"Next step to hit your goal by X..."
Analyst	Informational, neutral	Thoughtful & paced	"Attached is a detailed breakdown..."
Connector	Warm, personal	Flexible	"Just wanted to check in — how's life?"

Type	Tone	Timing	Language to Use
Supporter	Steady, gentle	Spread out & no pressure	"Here if you need me, no rush at all."

Use email automation that allows **manual tone customization** per recipient — not full rewrites, just slight shifts that keep your message aligned with their lens.

THE 80/20 RULE OF PERSONALIZATION

You don't need to personalize everything.

- ☑ **80%** of your content can stay the same (core offer, value, structure)

- ☑ **20%** gets flexed: tone, examples, CTA, and the opening

That 20% makes the difference between "meh" and "I feel like this was written for me."

ADD-ON TOOLS THAT HELP YOU FLEX FAST

Use tools that support dynamic personalization at scale:

- ☑ **CRM tags** for personality typing

- ☑ **Snippets & templates** that let you swap out tone/ phrasing

- ☑ **Video tools** (Loom, Vidyard) for personalized walkthroughs

- ☑ **ChatGPT** to adjust tone for each type (prompt: "Rewrite this message for a warm, relational tone")

FINAL THOUGHT

You don't need four sales strategies.

You need one **human strategy** — one that flexes with your buyer's lens, not your sales playbook.

When you know the person you're speaking to — their pace, their fears, their values — every message becomes more than a pitch.

It becomes a mirror.

And when someone sees themselves in your message, they don't just buy.

They believe you.

chapter 14

LET THEM BUY – ON THEIR TERMS

The best buying experiences aren't crafted in a vacuum — they're co-created with the buyer. When someone feels seen, heard, and respected, the path to "yes" becomes natural.

This chapter is about releasing control — and building frameworks that let buyers own the decision, with your guidance. You're not removing yourself from the sale. You're repositioning yourself as a trusted collaborator instead of a persuasive closer.

FROM PERSUASION TO PERMISSION

Traditional sales hinges on persuasion: overcoming objections, handling resistance, pushing urgency.

Modern sales invites participation: asking better questions, creating space, and providing clarity.

The old way: "Let me tell you why this is the best option." The new way: "Let's figure out what's right for you — together."

When you shift from convincing to empowering, trust follows.

BUYERS DON'T WANT SCRIPTS — THEY WANT OPTIONS

Buyers today don't want to be sold to. They want to be part of the process. They want to feel in control of their own decisions — especially in a world where so much feels out of their control.

Instead of saying, "Here's how we do it," try:

"Here are two paths that tend to work. Which one feels better to you?"

Instead of pushing a timeline, ask:

"What's a pace that feels right for this?"

Instead of guiding the call with a rigid script, use modular content blocks and real-time curiosity to build the narrative together.

Letting them lead doesn't mean you disappear. It means you become a trusted guide — not a pushy rep.

CHOICE IS A TRUST BUILDER

When buyers are allowed to:

- ☑ Choose their path
- ☑ Set their pace
- ☑ Ask questions without fear
- ☑ Express uncertainty

...they don't just feel more comfortable — they feel more in control.

And control, especially in uncertain times, is a currency. People don't always need to get their way — but they need to feel like they have a say.

Giving buyers autonomy reduces pressure, builds safety, and speeds up decision-making because they don't feel manipulated.

WHAT THIS LOOKS LIKE IN PRACTICE

Letting them buy on their terms doesn't mean becoming passive or losing structure. It means building space into your process.

Examples of Empowering Language:

- ☑ "You've got great instincts. I'm happy to share what's worked for others, but I trust you'll know what's best for your situation."

- ☑ "If it's helpful, I can lay out a couple of directions we could go — and you can let me know what feels most aligned."

- ☑ "We can adjust the timeline depending on what feels most manageable for your team."

Tactical Shifts:

- ☑ Offer clear choices without overwhelming

- ☑ Let the buyer "design" the solution with you

- ☑ Use language that invites, not corners

- ☑ Stay confident, but never controlling

- ☑ Allow time for reflection (especially for Supporters and Analysts)

- ☑ Honor relational momentum (especially for Connectors)

- ☑ Focus on destination, not details (especially for Drivers)

THIS DOESN'T MEAN YOU LOSE THE SALE

Letting them buy doesn't mean losing the sale — it often means closing it faster, with more confidence.

Buyers today want:

- ☑ **Safety** — emotionally and professionally

- ☑ **Clarity** — without pressure

- ☑ **Agency** — to own their choices

When you create a space where they can:

☑ Feel safe

☑ Think clearly

☑ Own the decision

…they don't just buy. They buy with commitment. They buy without regret. They buy and refer others.

This approach isn't passive. It's powerful.

Because when you stop trying to control the outcome, and start trusting the relationship — your buyers will do the same.

FINAL THOUGHT

Letting them buy isn't about stepping back. It's about stepping with them.

When you empower your buyers to feel in control, they lean in — not because you pushed, but because you partnered.

Next: How to bring this mindset to your entire team so it becomes a shared culture — not just a personal skill.

Chapter 15

HOW TO TEACH THIS TO YOUR TEAM

A great sales strategy means nothing if it stays locked in your head.

To create lasting change, the Let Them Buy mindset must live in your **culture** — not just in your top performers. When every team member understands how to meet people where they are, the results compound.

This chapter lays the groundwork for teaching, practicing, and scaling this mindset through practical training, live coaching, and a supportive sales environment.

STEP 1: TRAIN THE FRAMEWORK, NOT THE SCRIPT

Don't hand your team a script. Hand them a way to think.

Your reps should learn to:

- ☑ Identify buying personalities (Driver, Analyst, Connector, Supporter)
- ☑ Adapt communication style accordingly
- ☑ Prioritize buyer experience over seller agenda
- ☑ Embrace flexibility within structure

Scripts create robots. Frameworks create readiness.

Tip: Use scenario-based worksheets to help reps role-play different buyer types. Prompt them to respond in their own voice, guided by personality-aligned strategies.

STEP 2: TEACH LISTENING AS A CORE SKILL

Most teams train for pitch delivery. Your team should train for presence.

Teach your reps to:

- ☑ Listen for tone, energy shifts, and emotional cues

- ☑ Pause before responding — especially when objections arise

- ☑ Ask clarifying questions that show care and curiosity

Examples:

- ☑ "Sounds like there's some hesitation around timeline — can you say more about that?"

- ☑ "What would help this feel a bit easier to move forward on?"

Practice through active listening exercises. Use call recordings to highlight where emotional intelligence makes the difference.

STEP 3: INTEGRATE BUYER AWARENESS AT EVERY STAGE

Buyer-type awareness shouldn't be isolated to the discovery call. Embed it across:

- ☑ Email copy and tone

- ☑ Follow-up timing and method

- ☑ Proposal layout and detail level

- ☑ Objection handling

Examples:

- ☑ For **Drivers**, lead with outcomes and timelines

- ☑ For **Analysts**, provide structured breakdowns and optional resources

- ☑ For **Connectors**, personalize the follow-up and highlight shared values

- ☑ For **Supporters**, reiterate consistency and reduce urgency

Tool Idea: Include a "Buyer Type" field in your CRM to help reps track and tailor their communication over time.

STEP 4: USE DEBRIEFS AS COACHING MOMENTS

After every call or deal, go beyond "Did we win?" and ask:

- ☑ What type was this buyer?

- ☑ What signs made you think so?

- ☑ What worked — and what would you shift next time?

Use team huddles to share wins by personality type and review talk tracks.

Bonus: Create worksheet prompts for self-assessment and reflection after each major deal.

STEP 5: CELEBRATE BUYER-CENTERED WINS

If you want to reinforce a culture of buyer-first selling, reward the behavior — not just the outcome.

Shout out team members who:

- ☑ Adapted their communication to meet the buyer's pace

- ☑ Practiced patience with a hesitant Supporter

- ☑ Built trust with a skeptical Analyst

- ☑ Respected boundaries while following up with a Connector

Make emotional intelligence and adaptability as valued as revenue closed.

STEP 6: LEAD IT FROM THE TOP

Culture shifts start with leadership. Your team will do what you model.

Ask yourself:

- ☑ Do I coach differently based on personality?

- ☑ Do I slow down for understanding, or speed up for numbers?

- ☑ Do I create room for learning and growth, or only room for performance?

Modeling empathy, active listening, and autonomy invites your team to do the same with prospects.

Leadership Worksheet: Create prompts that help leaders reflect on their coaching styles and how they adjust for different sales personalities.

BUILDING THE COURSE AND WORKSHEETS

To support your rollout of this methodology:

- ☑ **Build a course** with modules that mirror the buyer types, outreach strategy, and follow-up framework

- ☑ **Include worksheets** for:

    - ⊘ Practicing tone matching

    - ⊘ Identifying buyer cues

- ✓ Writing sample follow-ups per personality

- ✓ Mapping real prospects into each category

☑ **Use group role-play** to reinforce learning in safe, structured environments

If you don't have the time or internal bandwidth to build these materials yourself, I offer a done-for-you option where I'll create the custom course and worksheets tailored to your team, industry, and sales environment. This allows you to roll out the Let Them Buy system quickly and effectively — with materials designed to stick.

FINAL THOUGHT

Teaching your team to "let them buy" isn't about making them passive. It's about making them powerful — because they're equipped with the mindset, tools, and self-awareness to lead sales conversations with empathy and adaptability.

And when your entire team knows how to do that? You stop managing sales. You start **multiplying trust**.

And that's when real scale begins.

Epilogue

THE REAL WIN

The world doesn't need more closers. It needs more **openers** — people who open conversations, open minds, and open doors for others to buy in ways that feel good, clear, and real.

You don't have to sell harder. You just have to listen better, see clearer, and show up more human.

This book isn't the end — it's a starting point.

WHAT YOU'VE BUILT

If you've made it this far, you've done more than read. You've committed to:

- ☑ Respecting the buyer's pace

- ☑ Listening before responding

- ☑ Speaking to people as whole human beings

- ☑ Making space for others to choose instead of being pushed

That puts you in rare company. In a world obsessed with urgency, you've chosen to build trust.

THE LEGACY OF A BUYER-FIRST MINDSET

Letting people buy on their terms isn't just a technique. It's a **philosophy** — one that changes how you show up in every part of your business.

It creates clients who stick around. It builds referrals that don't have to be chased. It makes selling feel less like a performance — and more like a relationship.

And when you do it consistently, it creates a brand that people trust.

WHAT COMES NEXT

If this book helped you rethink how sales should work, the next step is learning how to apply it to every personality type you encounter.

My follow-up book —

Stop Selling, Let Them Buy: The Personality Playbook

— is your tactical guide to navigating buyer behavior through the lens of emotional intelligence, personality science, and sales psychology.

It's packed with insights, frameworks, and ready-to-use strategies to help you and your team connect faster, build trust sooner, and close more deals — all without ever sounding like you're "selling." Available now wherever this book is sold.

PHILIP VIVIER

Thank You

If you've made it this far — thank you.

You care about your craft. You care about your clients. You believe that sales can be relational, not just transactional.

And that's what sets you apart.

Now go out there and **let them buy**.

With clarity, compassion, and confidence.

Acknowledgements

To every client, colleague, and team member who ever said, "That's not how I buy" — thank you. You pushed this thinking forward.

To the companies that trusted me to help shape their approach — and let me teach this work before it had a name — I'm grateful.

To my family, who reminded me that empathy doesn't end when the workday does — you're the heartbeat behind everything I write.

To my early mentors and sounding boards who challenged me to clarify my thinking and backed me even when the path wasn't clear — your belief made this possible.

And to every reader looking for a better way — I see you. Let them buy. On their terms. And lead the way by how you show up.

Thank you for being part of this journey.

— Philip